GW01006181

A GIFT FOR:

_____

FROM:

_____

DATE:

_____

Crazy About My Grandparents

BARBOUR
PUBLISHING

CRAZY ABOUT MY GRANDPARENTS™

COPYRIGHT © 2003 BY MARK GILROY COMMUNICATIONS, INC.
TULSA, OKLAHOMA

ART AND DESIGN BY JACKSON DESIGN COMPANY
SILOAM SPRINGS, ARKANSAS

ISBN 1-58660-847-9

ALL RIGHTS RESERVED. NO PART OF THIS PUBLICATION MAY
BE REPRODUCED OR TRANSMITTED IN ANY FORM OR BY ANY MEANS
WITHOUT WRITTEN PERMISSION OF THE PUBLISHER.

SCRIPTURE QUOTATIONS ARE TAKEN FROM THE *HOLY BIBLE,*
NEW LIVING TRANSLATION, COPYRIGHT © 1996. USED BY
PERMISSION OF TYNDALE HOUSE PUBLISHERS, INC.,
WHEATON, ILLINOIS 60189. ALL RIGHTS RESERVED.

PUBLISHED BY BARBOUR PUBLISHING, INC., P.O. BOX 719,
UHRICHSVILLE, OHIO 44683, www.barbourpublishing.com

Member of the
Evangelical Christian
Publishers Association

PRINTED IN CHINA.
5 4 3 2 1

Thank You!

THANK YOU FOR BEING
A GREAT EXAMPLE
OF INTEGRITY, WISDOM,
AND FUN FOR ME!
YOU ARE THE GREATEST
~ AND I LOVE YOU!

I'M CRAZY ABOUT MY GRANDPA
BECAUSE HE GETS ME OUT OF TROUBLE
WITH MY DAD BY TELLING WHAT
<u>HE</u> DID WHEN HE WAS MY AGE.

I'M CRAZY ABOUT MY GRANDMA
BECAUSE SHE LOVES THE MALL
AS MUCH AS I DO!

I'M CRAZY ABOUT MY GRANDPARENTS
BECAUSE THEY STILL HAVE TONS
OF GET-UP-AND-GO.

I'M CRAZY ABOUT MY GRANDPA
BECAUSE HE LOVES TO STAY UP LATE
AND WATCH SCARY MOVIES WITH ME.

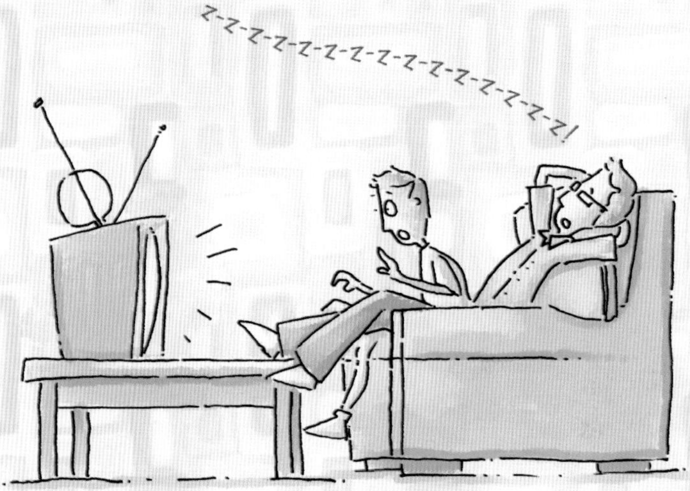

I'M CRAZY ABOUT MY GRANDMA
BECAUSE SHE LOOKS SO YOUNG.

I'M CRAZY ABOUT MY GRANDPARENTS
BECAUSE THEY LOOK KIND OF CUTE
WHEN THEY KISS.

I'M CRAZY ABOUT MY GRANDPA
BECAUSE HE BUYS US
THREE SCOOPS OF ICE CREAM.

I'M CRAZY ABOUT MY GRANDMA
BECAUSE SHE LOVES MY ARTWORK.

I'M CRAZY ABOUT MY GRANDPARENTS
BECAUSE THEY ALWAYS PUT SOMETHING
SPECIAL IN MY BIRTHDAY CARD.

(AND THEY DON'T CARE IF I DON'T
READ THE MESSAGE FIRST.)

I'M CRAZY ABOUT MY GRANDPA
BECAUSE HE MAKES
THE BEST BREAKFASTS.

I'M CRAZY ABOUT MY GRANDMA
BECAUSE SHE GIVES GREAT HUGS.

I'M CRAZY ABOUT MY GRANDPARENTS
BECAUSE THEY LISTEN TO COOL MUSIC.

I'M CRAZY ABOUT MY GRANDPA
BECAUSE HE DOESN'T CALL SOMEBODY
ELSE WHEN HE FIXES THINGS.

I'M CRAZY ABOUT MY GRANDMA
BECAUSE SHE ALWAYS PICKS OUT
THE PERFECT CHRISTMAS PRESENT.

I'M CRAZY ABOUT MY GRANDPARENTS
BECAUSE I KNOW THEY GET SAD WHEN WE
CAN'T GO ON VACATION WITH THEM.

So, have I ever told you the one about the...?

I'M CRAZY ABOUT MY GRANDPA
BECAUSE HE TELLS FUNNY JOKES
THAT MAKE EVERYBODY LAUGH.

I'M CRAZY ABOUT MY GRANDMA
BECAUSE SHE DOESN'T SWEAT
THE SMALL STUFF.

I'M CRAZY ABOUT MY GRANDPARENTS
BECAUSE THEY REALLY KNOW HOW
TO GET INTO THE CHRISTMAS SPIRIT.

I'M CRAZY ABOUT MY GRANDPA
BECAUSE HE HARDLY EVER
HAS "SENIOR MOMENTS"!

I'M CRAZY ABOUT MY GRANDMA
BECAUSE SHE FIXES EXOTIC MEALS
WE NEVER HAVE AT MY HOUSE.

I'M CRAZY ABOUT MY GRANDPARENTS
BECAUSE THEIR PHOTO ALBUMS ARE
BIGGER — AND EVEN HAVE NEAT STUFF
LIKE BLACK AND WHITE PICTURES.

I'M CRAZY ABOUT MY GRANDPA
BECAUSE HE IS MY BIGGEST FAN!

I'M CRAZY ABOUT MY GRANDMA
BECAUSE SHE INSPIRES ME
TO BE A GOOD READER.

I'M CRAZY ABOUT MY GRANDPARENTS
BECAUSE THEY HAVE
A SECRET WAY OF SAVING MONEY
EVERYWHERE THEY GO.

I'M CRAZY ABOUT MY GRANDPA
BECAUSE HE ACTS LIKE A KID!

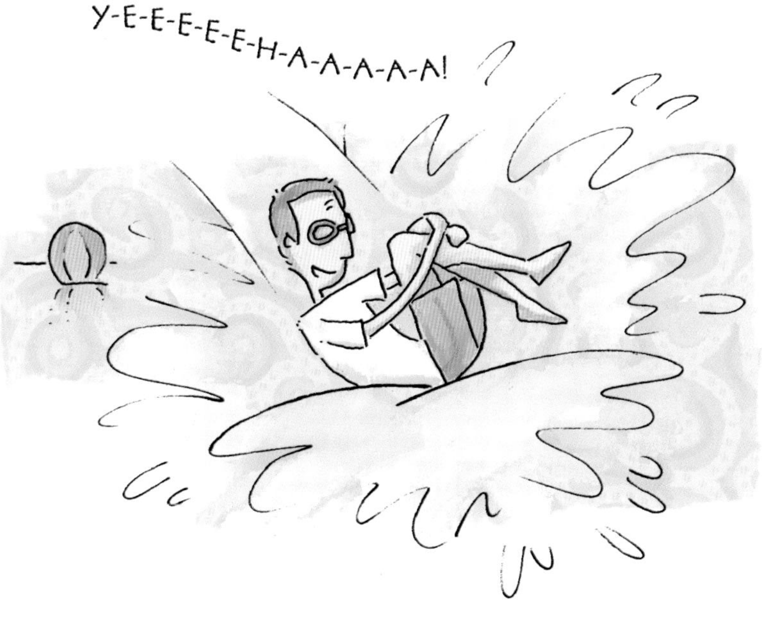
Y-E-E-E-E-E-H-A-A-A-A-A!

I'M CRAZY ABOUT MY GRANDMA
BECAUSE HER HOUSE IS FULL
OF WONDERFUL AROMAS.

I'M CRAZY ABOUT MY GRANDPARENTS
BECAUSE THEY HAVE
COOL GAMES AT THEIR HOUSE
THAT DON'T NEED BATTERIES.

I'M CRAZY ABOUT MY GRANDPA
BECAUSE HE REMEMBERS
THE GOOD OLD DAYS.

I'M CRAZY ABOUT MY GRANDMA
BECAUSE SHE KNOWS HOW TO MAKE
A BAD DAY GET BETTER.

I'M CRAZY ABOUT MY GRANDPARENTS
BECAUSE THEY HAVE THE
COOLEST STUFF IN THEIR ATTIC.

I'M CRAZY ABOUT MY GRANDPA
BECAUSE HE STAYS IN GREAT SHAPE
BY TAKING LONG WALKS.

Oh.....Just what I wanted.

I'M CRAZY ABOUT MY GRANDMA
BECAUSE SHE IS EASY
TO BUY GIFTS FOR.

I'M CRAZY ABOUT MY GRANDPARENTS
BECAUSE THEY GAVE ME
A GREAT PARENT.

I'M CRAZY ABOUT MY GRANDPA
BECAUSE HE'S STILL PRETTY STRONG
FOR AN OLD GUY.

I'M CRAZY ABOUT MY GRANDMA
BECAUSE SHE WILL
NEVER LET US STARVE.

I'M CRAZY ABOUT MY GRANDPARENTS
BECAUSE THEY ARE
INCREDIBLY CONNECTED.

I'M CRAZY ABOUT MY GRANDPA
BECAUSE HE DOESN'T GET
STRESSED OUT BY LIFE.

I'M CRAZY ABOUT MY GRANDMA
BECAUSE SHE'S WAY TOO CREATIVE
TO EVER GET OLD.

I'M CRAZY ABOUT MY GRANDPARENTS
BECAUSE EVEN THOUGH THEY HAVE
OLD-FASHIONED VALUES,
THEY ARE VERY COOL!

I think this will be enough for now~
be sure to come by next year, too!

I'M CRAZY ABOUT MY GRANDPA BECAUSE HE KNOWS HOW TO HANDLE PESKY DOOR-TO-DOOR SALESPEOPLE.

I'M CRAZY ABOUT MY GRANDMA
BECAUSE SHE UNDERSTANDS
WHAT I'M FEELING EVEN BETTER
THAN OTHER KIDS MY AGE.

I'M CRAZY ABOUT MY GRANDPARENTS
BECAUSE THEY KNOW GRANDKIDS NEED
SOMEONE TO PRAY FOR THEM.

I'M CRAZY ABOUT MY GRANDPA BECAUSE
HE TEACHES WHAT IS RIGHT THROUGH
HIS ACTIONS, NOT JUST HIS WORDS.

Now take it to the neighbors three doors down—they just had a baby last week.

I'M CRAZY ABOUT MY GRANDMA
BECAUSE SHE KNOWS HOW
TO MAKE PEOPLE FEEL BETTER.

I'M CRAZY ABOUT MY GRANDPARENTS
BECAUSE THEY ARE CRAZY ABOUT ME.

I'M CRAZY ABOUT MY GRANDPARENTS BECAUSE THEY ARE THE GREATEST!

EVERY TIME I THINK OF YOU, I GIVE THANKS TO MY GOD.

PHILIPPIANS 1:3 NLT